Terry John Woods'

New Farmhouse Style

Terry John Woods'

New Farmhouse Style

Written with Dale West

Photographs by Kindra Clineff

Stewart, Tabori & Chang, New York

Published in 2009 by Stewart, Tabori & Chang
An imprint of ABRAMS

Text copyright © 2009 by Terry John Woods
Photographs copyright © 2009 by Kindra Clineff

Library of Congress Cataloging-in-Publication Data:
Woods, Terry John.
  Terry John Woods' new farmhouse style / by Terry John Woods;
photographs by Kindra Clineff. p. cm.
  ISBN 978-1-58479-792-0 (alk. paper)
  1. Farmhouses–Decoration–United States. 2. Interior decoration
–United States. I. Clineff, Kindra. II. Title. III. Title:
New farmhouse style.
  NK2195.R87W67 2009   747–dc22   2009002263

Editor: Dervla Kelly
Designer: Tim Preston
Production Manager: Tina Cameron

The text of this book was composed in Garamond and Futura.

Printed and bound in China.
10 9 8 7 6 5 4 3 2

THE ART OF BOOKS SINCE 1949
115 West 18th Street
New York, NY 10011
www.abramsbooks.com

Contents

Introduction

Mention Vermont to anyone and you are sure to spark memories, perceptions, and experiences unique to each individual. Likewise, the definition of "farmhouse" is certain to range from the details of an architectural style to the emotions evoked by the slap of a screen door on a hot summer day.

"New farmhouse style" is as difficult to define. In this book I'll share some design ideas that are simple, affordable, and timeless.

Growing up in Vermont, on my family's farm, I learned how to work hard, use what we had on hand, and care for the land that sustained us. During those years I also developed an appreciation for design, simplicity, and the natural beauty that surrounded us. I believe that we should live well with the cherished items in our homes and discover the potential and promise hidden in everyday objects. It is possible to both respect and reinvent heirlooms, antiques, and other treasured possessions.

Grandmother's ladder-back chair deserves to be treated like fine art, so why should it not hang on the wall? An old chicken feeder from the barn realizes new potential as a stylish plate rack. Old windows come inside, while old doors adorn the garden.

New Farmhouse Style offers a fresh look at an old object, a sense of style where it may often be overlooked, and simple design ideas that you can use in your own home.

It is important to remember that this is not a *how-to* or a *recipe* book, but rather a *what-if* book. A recipe book will tell you what ingredients to use, when to mix, when to blend, and what temperature to use. A how-to book will give you the exact measurements for building a closet. Some decorating books will follow suit and tempt you into re-creating specific vignettes and design schemes. But this one asks, What if you took these ideas and decorated with the things you love and that bring you comfort? This book shows you how to bring favorite ingredients into your home design and create your own recipe for living well.

Chapter 1

Creating Personal Comfort

Living well means knowing what brings you comfort. For some it may be a
bouquet from the garden, or perhaps mementos framed and hanging on the
wall, while others will find solace in detail and order. Allow your personal
comfort to grow and fill your home.

Make a large family room more intimate by personalizing it with things you love. Here, formal wing chairs are softened with blue toile down pillows. Casual placements of items, such as an old seascape print on the floor against the cupboard and a favorite chalky white cement garden statue, add a personal touch. Natural sunlight showcases the room.

When I was growing up, the second floor of my family's farmhouse had no heat of its own. We relied on heat from the woodstove downstairs to climb the stairs and keep us warm even on the coldest Vermont nights. My father would feed the fire a few times in the night to ward off the cold, but by morning, when my siblings and I needed to get up and help him in the barn, we couldn't dress quickly enough nor scurry fast enough to the warmth of the stove downstairs.

Yet somewhere between waking and that mad rush, I recall a feeling that later became my founding definition for personal comfort: The blankets are piled high and toasty warm. The house is quiet except for the sound of my father taking wood from the wood box and opening the stove door to feed the embers. Within seconds, the smell of wood smoke drifts up the stairs. I hear my father walking through the house until the back door latches, and I know he has begun his day. Another hour of slumber is mine. When he returns, his footsteps fall harder; he is less mindful of our sleep when tending the stove. Pots and pans clank; my mother begins to wake the kitchen. By the time the smell of breakfast has reached the top of the stairs, so have we. Our day has begun. This is my personal comfort.

We have all experienced moments when we are more than just comfortable, we are safe, warm, and part of something bigger. Later in life, when a situation resonates in the same way, these feelings return just as if we have another hour of warm slumber under the covers. Decorating your home or garden is really about creating opportunities to feel this sense of personal comfort. For some it may be a sun-drenched chair and a good book, for others it may be a garden bench overlooking a favorite perennial. The emotion is there, and you will know when it is stirred. Creating personal comfort is an inside job. No one else can do it for you, nor would you want them to.

The objects you surround yourself with play an important role in creating comfort; they usually work on several sensory levels. For me, there is a tricky balance between a piece being visually pleasing and functional. It is one thing to find a chair that is a work of art. It is another to find one that is as comfortable as it is beautiful. Remember, there is no need to compromise one for the other. Take time looking for the piece that appeals to more than one of your senses. Surprise yourself. You are much more apt to come across the perfect piece for your home when shopping with your senses rather than a list.

A number of elements help me create my own personal comfort. They may or may not resonate with you. I love color. This sounds strange coming from someone who has painted an entire interior white, but by doing so, I allowed the colors from our gardens to explode into the house. Nature's changing colors are far more interesting and diverse than anything I could ever hope to create with a wall treatment. The color accents of cut flowers, the subtle shades of white, and the mosaic effect of furniture with chipping layers of paint all lend to the comforting effect of color.

I also enjoy texture. Contrast is created by pairing the rough surface of stone with the smooth finish of ironstone plates or the aged surface of hand-hewn beams with homespun fabric. Rich textures offer tactile as well as visual comfort. Experiment with textures. You may discover that their contrast heightens your awareness of decorative elements previously overlooked.

Finally, I value provenance, for it is both personal and powerful. A family piece with a long history may offer new meaning to each generation. I have a rocking chair that my grandmother bought when I was born. She insisted first on a piece that had just the right amount of rock. The personal comfort she found in the chair was made complete when her newborn grandchild lay in her arms. Needless to say, those loving hours of rocking are now a part of that chair; I only need to sit in it to know. Use those personal items as they were meant to be used. Let them tell you of their larger history. There is personal comfort in knowing.

There are also elements of form, scale, and design that are part of creating personal comfort: when, for example, a table is just the right size and design or when the rosebush offers the right amount of height, texture, and color. These considerations are individual, and therein lies the foundation for developing personal comfort; it has to be done for you, by you. If it feels right, it can't be wrong!

The kitchen has always been the center of a home and should be decorated as such. Here, a warm breeze from the back garden and late afternoon sun fill the room. The large antique French baker's table, centered in the long space, displays a weathered iron urn filled with fall hydrangea, making the room look and feel as inviting and personal as any in the house.

The crisp blue in the striped tablecloth pops when combined with a stack of white ironstone bowls. The white canvas barrel-back chair, with its blue pillow, harmonizes the area.

A bouquet of purple lilacs brings an unexpected splash of color and the sweet smell of spring to any room in the house. Fresh flowers add a relaxing feel to a hectic work area or home office. Remember to take a break and smell the lilacs!

Sometimes a simple cupboard display is made more interesting by what peeks from behind the door. This collection of Victorian ironstone sugar bowls lures the eye, beckoning further investigation.

Flowers are a great way to personalize any space with color and fragrance. Here, peony blooms are grouped in a simple bowl on an old tarnished silver tray. Because the table and sofa are centered in the room, the flowers can be enjoyed from all angles.

Most farmhouse kitchens were large, with an informal dining area. The eating nook in this one is a special place to sit, relax, and reflect alone, and is also perfect for a quick lunch for two or a social cup of tea. If not for the clock on the wall, time might just slow down a bit.

Paired with everyday mixing bowls, a yellow and white English milk pitcher displays flowers on a kitchen shelf. The blend of texture and color brings a sense of unexpected style to this otherwise utilitarian work area.

Luscious Turkish towels blanket the wall into the bathroom. A 1950s veneered sideboard, freshly painted in several shades of white, has new life as a vanity. A vessel sink paired with an Italian faucet mounted on the vanity creates an interesting blend of finishes, as well as a collaboration of contemporary and vintage styles. The result is easy on the eye and soothing to body and soul.

Creating order in selected areas of your home may offer respite from more cluttered areas in your life. Here in the bedroom, down pillows covered in percale cotton cases are casually stacked on the bed. Similar hues harmonize to achieve a relaxing feeling, but different mix-and-match colors could also be used.

▶ An old commode, a pine grange hall table, and a slipcovered chair create a special sitting area in the light-filled sunroom. Cherished items, such as handmade Santas, a grouping of white poinsettias, a folksy portrait, and a warm patchwork throw, let you relax and appreciate your personalized space. The texture and design of the beadboard ceiling and buttery pine floors combine nicely to add to the comforting feel of the room.

▼ Colorful daisies in a small ironstone pitcher highlight the muted tones of the early wooden mantel and nautical print. The contrasting textures and fragrant blossoms make this a multisensory vignette.

▲ Different collectibles create interest when paired in areas that are undressed and plain. This Victorian child's shoe takes center stage atop an architectural detail with a crackled finish. The two items work together because of size, patina, and color. These little wooden corbels are handy displays for small items deserving the center of attention. Not only do they bring a piece to the forefront, they allow it to be easily changed out.

▲ The tidy order of the distressed seashells against the antique French cotton ticking rivals a display of fine crystal and silver candlesticks while bringing something cherished to the table.

◄ Making a room cozy with your personal items can reach beyond the bedroom and other private spaces. Here, the dining room becomes a showcase for just such items. A collection of ironstone platters hangs like fine art on the white textured walls. Recently gathered seashells accent fresh limelight hydrangeas arranged in a large water pitcher on the table. The end result is an inexpensive but surprisingly charming display.

Three European flowerpots filled with scented geraniums dress up a workstation in the kitchen. The clean lines of the counter space and stainless appliances welcome the color, textures, and scents from the early spring plants. Displayed on a platter, they are easily moved when space is needed or when their color and scent could freshen up another room.

A formal Victorian chair takes on a new life after being painted and covered with organic white linen, dramatically simplifying its ornate lines. Combined with a salmon-colored amaryllis and a dog garden ornament, the sitting space speaks of a hopeful spring day in the dead of winter. The strong hues of the blooming flower and bold stripe of the down pillow add vibrant color to an otherwise drab space.

Aromatic rosemary topiaries dress up an old English pine tray on a white distressed coffee table. The newly painted white flowerpots spruce up the old table—a yard sale find—giving the area a fresh, clean feel.

◀ Spending my entire life in a farmhouse with only one large closet has been challenging. Creating storage that doesn't look like storage is always at the top of my to-do list. In the bedroom, wicker baskets and trunks are stacked one upon the other, according to size. The largest holds heavy or bulky items not regularly used. The top basket is perfect for smaller, more frequently used items, such as television remotes and writing stationery.

▲ The bedroom is probably the most used private space in the house, so creating a comfort there that allows you to settle down and relax is essential. The monochrome color scheme in this bedroom soothes the eye; the sparse décor doesn't distract from contemplative thought. The mixing of different styles, such as the modern lamps and fabrics juxtaposed with the primitive blanket box and antique French lead frieze over the bed, creates an inviting space. There is texture and warmth, yet the surroundings are uncomplicated and refreshing after a long, stressful day.

▼ Creating playful areas throughout the home makes you smile to see them, no matter how frequently you happen upon them. I started making teddy bears and selling them worldwide twenty years ago, and have always included them in my design schemes. Made from English and German mohair, these one-of-a-kind bears are jointed and stuffed with excelsior just as their ancestors would have been. Here, a teddy rides a tricycle on the front porch and welcomes all who enter the house.

▲ My handmade teddy bears are always somewhere in the farmhouse. A foursome of my latest creations are lined up in sequence on the floor, ready to be named and shipped off to their new homes.

◀ A distressed teddy sits on antique parade bunting during a summer holiday celebration. Creating themed personal spaces, especially during seasonal get-togethers with family and friends, is a great way to share your passion for collections while showcasing your cherished items in a different and fun way.

▶ A favorite family rocking horse gives a gentle ride to a center-seamed mohair teddy bear. The two collectibles make a great whimsical pairing that can be enjoyed daily. Remember, your favorite things are what make your personal space yours, so bring them out for all to see.

▶Layers of rich cotton and linen, mixed and matched for colors and textures, make the bedroom area seem more individual and cottagelike. Pillows piled high add to the relaxation and peaceful comfort the bed promises.

▶Paperwhite blooms in a small, white earthenware cup rest on an early English transferware plate. The trio displays appealing tone-on-tone whites, and the smooth textures of both plate and cup mimic the delicate texture of the petals. The floral transfer patterns and scent of the flowers are added perks.

▶Contrasting paint finishes can be very effective, especially when mixing aged, distressed finishes with newly painted ones. Old paint faded to a soothing shade of blue graces this cottage pine bureau in the bedroom. The white Regency mirror complements the distressed reproduction sleigh bed and looks as if it was made to pair with the bureau. The overall feel is airy and restful, as a bedroom should be.

No two things are alike in this attic bedroom, yet the space works as a whole. A section of picket fence found roadside and now decorated with a blueberry twig wreath reigns over the bed as a headboard. The bedside stands differ in height and style, and are adorned with a medley of old china, baskets, and dried flowers. The handmade folk art sheep rests against the stacks of down pillows. Eclectic groupings such as these can create a cozy atmosphere in any space.

Resting on a table in the mudroom, a plain white bowl holds a single peony blossom. You immediately smell the fragrance and experience a sense of peacefulness when you enter the house.

In the den, an old wooden rocking horse sits on a tabletop corralled by stacks of books and garden-themed items.

This Victorian pressed-back oak chair is from a set of four that has been in my family for years. Given away to other family members from time to time, they always find their way back home. Now the set has been artistically slipcovered in broadcloth, giving them a more casual and contemporary feel. As you can see, slipcovers aren't just for upholstered furniture; try covering tables, headboards, even blanket boxes. Remember to prepare the fabric by washing it in hot water and drying it at a high temperature before the slipcovers are constructed. This will guarantee a perfect fit after many years of washings.

◀ French chairs loosely slipcovered in painter's cloth anchor the corners of the small farmhouse den. The casual feel is accomplished through the use of similar tones of white paint on the walls and floor, the linen Roman shade, and the newly painted silver storage chest separating the chairs. Unexpected items, such as the old cracked porch column and trio of pearl seashells, make this area more personal and interesting.

▶ Patterns and blends of fabric work well together when they are similar in shade and hue. Here, a wide-striped chair works well with a similarly striped pillow and a busy patchwork quilt.

The regulation of natural light plays an important role in planning a personal space. Here, brilliant sunlight pours through multiple windows and saturates the camelback sofa. The bright area is perfect for reading a favorite book or taking a warm mid-afternoon nap. Bedrooms or offices may require darkening shades to diffuse the light or prevent it from entering, keeping the room peaceful and workable.

Morning sun gleams over the bed in the guestroom. Overnight visitors will appreciate, in any season, the freshly washed, high-quality linens, down pillows, and a breathable down comforter.

Art is welcome in any room of the house. These botanical prints have been sorted by size and color, and are ready to be framed and hung on the wall. By grouping according to color and subject and using similarly toned frames, you can cluster many photographs together and have them work as a whole.

Chapter 2

Bringing the Inside Out

Your home extends well beyond the walls of your house. Nature's colors, textures, fragrances, and forms become new elements of design when introduced to your inside living space. Likewise, heirloom objects and other collected treasures expand your home when brought outside to your yard and garden.

I remember in my youth returning home after a long, hot day of cutting hay to enjoy the cooling temperatures of the early evening. We would frequently drag the old farm table and chairs outside to dine. Today, both the table and the tradition still exist. Dressed simply with ironstone pitchers and fresh flowers from the garden, it provides the perfect setting for dining outside.

A warm March day in Vermont is a welcome visitor. Its brilliant sunlight melts snow and warms sod, hinting of things to come, yet it quickly slips away upon the arrival of a crisp, clear night, leaving us at winter's mercy for a few weeks more. It is no wonder, then, that in the first days of spring, doors and windows are thrown open to the fresh air and sunshine. Suddenly clotheslines sag under a colorful array of laundry and linens flapping in the breeze. The days linger on the sheets and invite a special kind of sleep. Spring peepers, knowing what is to come, celebrate each night as if it were the first. We want to hold on to spring as long as we can. It was a promised reward for bearing the long, cold winter, and we have earned it.

The anticipation of spring is longer than the season itself. Spring is so fleeting; don't let it go unsung! In these early days, the house can be a surrogate for the garden that still sleeps outdoors. For as long as I can remember, we have kept bulbs in the freezer over winter and then nestled them in clay pots, allowing them to gently warm on the windowsill. They bloom well before Mother Nature would allow such a display in her garden. Paperwhites are eager growers and readily available. Tulips and Tête-à-tête daffodils are also easily forced. A wander around the barren yard might yield branches from the apple tree or shoots from the forsythia. These can be cut, refrigerated, and coaxed into bloom a few weeks before

they appear outside, creating a celebration of spring with their fragrant blossoms of pink, white, and vibrant yellow.

As the days warm and summer settles in, we find ourselves outside earlier in the day and later at night. Breakfast may be taken on the porch, lunch enjoyed by the pond, and dinner shared on the back deck overlooking the gardens. Our living space grows beyond the confines of the house as I bring favorite objects from the house to the garden or yard. Being intentional and creative about my choices is fun and rewarding. A table, bureau, or chairs can be handy outside while also creating a pleasing, unexpected focus against nature's backdrop of color and design. The farm table that serves us so well in the dining room every winter joins us in the yard. Kitchen chairs circle the garden fireplace, where we rely on the flames to extend our day by just a few more hours.

The backyard garden is also well represented inside, with cut flowers adorning every room. The bowl on the kitchen table is filled with the bounty of the vegetable garden. This is summer! Inside and out have merged. We want to enjoy every moment, so we embrace it. We spend as much time as we possibly can outside, and when we must come in, we bring it with us!

A summer garden dinner party is a perfect opportunity to enjoy the season in the company of friends. The candles on the table flicker like fireflies. The outdoor grill allows easy conversation with friends while cooking and is not unlike the use of summer kitchens of the past when the indoor kitchen was just too hot. We all enjoy the evening and move inside only when the dew cools the air and the embers in the fire start to fade. Good friends, good food, a spectacular summer night. These are the times to cherish.

As the summer begins to fade, the days get shorter and the evening chill drives us back inside. Early fall colors are foreshadowed in the garden's yellow squash, blueberries, blackberries, and bright red tomatoes. The smell of apples, dried leaves, and a wood fire hangs in the air. As squirrels and chipmunks carry the fall harvest into their homes, we, too, gather our favorite outdoor things and bring them in to enjoy. Antique garden statuary and iron urns serve as unique accents throughout the house. Decorating with pumpkins, apples, colorful mums, and bittersweet captures the essence of autumn. Enjoy it while you can. Soon, winter will be with us again.

As the snow begins to fall and the holiday season comes upon us, we are once again stirred by the need to gather treasures from outside. Greens, twigs, and sundry berries bring life to our rooms. Trees and wreaths are a central part of holiday decorating but do not have to disappear in January. A live evergreen will remain vibrant and healthy when properly potted. And while Mother Nature's palette dims, we lend her a hand, brightening our yard and garden with colorful lights and glittering decorations. Having the colors and smells of nature in our homes during this season of short, bright days and long, dark nights reminds us of the seasons to follow this quiet time.

Then one morning we awake and sense a subtle yet palpable change. The buckets stored all winter inside the sugarhouses of Vermont magically appear, hugging the maple trees. Windows open, one by one, and early bulbs send up their shoots. Spring has kept her promise. Our welcome guest has returned.

◀ Next to the garden workstation, an unimportant attic-find bureau rests outside, weathering from the elements. Used to house garden tools, flowerpots, frogs, and vases, such a bureau is a must-have. Everything is at your fingertips—no need to venture inside in muddy boots.

▶ A beachcomber's seashell becomes a delicate vase for spring paperwhite blossoms. Just fill it with water, add your favorite small blooms, and display it in a special place in your home.

▼ Used as a garden pedestal, an old farm milk can holds a transferware pitcher full of meadow buttercups. In off-season months, it has the same use inside the house.

◤ Even a favorite nonwatertight item can become a fabulous vase. Here, an old splint basket lined with a glass baking dish holds a variety of brightly colored daylilies. This portable display can be rotated around the house or carried off to your next neighborhood potluck dinner.

Let the fresh air in! After months of winter, nothing is more pleasing than filling the house with the warm breath of spring. Canvas slipcovers on wing chairs dance in the breeze. The wonderful fragrance of crabapple blossoms pervades the room. Rooster, our golden retriever, guards the patio to make sure no unwanted chipmunks enter.

▶ Painter's cloth was a wonderful and durable way to slipcover these inexpensive yard-sale chairs from a motel. Standing in a row of four beside the pond, the sturdy and functional chairs are fun garden art. Though not weather-durable, they make a mild sunny day more enjoyable with their unpretentious comfort.

◀ The east wall of the old milk house now serves as a backdrop for the garden workstation just outside the house. Rows of shovels line the wall, ready to serve. An old farm table and bench stand ready for potting plants or creating the perfect summer flower arrangement. Not only is this workstation visually appealing, it is ever useful for a variety of needs.

The green and white Victorian "ice water" pitcher finds a new purpose on a casual dining table outside holding mismatched silverware for the upcoming meal. An attractive, useful addition to the table, the pitcher is also easy to carry. It will certainly be enjoyed in this manner for many years to come.

A large green garden urn is handy just inside the front door where it can hold such items as umbrellas, firewood, or winter gloves and hats. It is also appreciated just as it is. Garden statuary and other outdoor ornaments work beautifully inside during the winter months, reminding us that the gardening season is coming.

Yellow buttercups are set off by a blue and white linen dish-towel on the service table next to the grill. Visually pleasing as a small table runner, the towel is also within arm's reach for an accidental spill.

I'll decorate with anything available. Fruits, such as lemons or apples, look great in a bowl anywhere in the house before they are used in the kitchen. Garden vegetables also offer a variety of colors and textures. Here in the dining room, garden squash becomes an eye-catching totem pole with its splash of bright colors and can be enjoyed for weeks. Try setting a bowl of string beans or a couple of ripe tomatoes on a small cutting board on your kitchen counter. The possibilities are endless.

A collection of old medicinal bottles hanging on the back door serves as a cluster vase. A beckoning welcome, the bottles clang together when the door opens, announcing the arrival of guests. Used here for fall flowers, this unique door decoration might display balsam twigs, spring blooms, or even small flags as the seasons and holidays change.

▶Shapes have always made a strong statement in decorating. Here, where the colors of the walls and furniture are kept to a bare minimum, shapes command the room. They immediately draw the eye, demanding that attention be paid to the pleasing silhouettes and textures throughout the room.

▲A copper eagle weather vane, rich in verdigris, rests upon a distressed white finial. Once mounted high on a barn roof, the vane now perches over the coffee table book collection in the den. Never polish verdigris copper such as this; it will lessen the object's value and mar its appearance.

▲An old white post office cubby now hangs from the side of the house near the garden. The nooks make a great showcase for small outdoor collectibles or flower arrangements such as these ironstone cups filled with buttercups. Try flowerpots, bird nests, seashells, or a favorite rock collection.

By the back door of the farmhouse is an old stone wall. It is sort of a catchall resting place for everything from rows of seedlings waiting to be planted to the nightly harvest from the vegetable garden. Here, an auction purchase of ironstone (to be added to my over-the-top collection) rests on the wall. They will be washed and left on the stones for a few more days to dry and be appreciated as garden art.

◀ Not everything has to be old or tell a fantastic family story. The pair of garden ornaments gracing the side table in the living room were bought new. With their appealing color and texture, they added interest to the lavender garden for many years. Today they are used inside in a more formal setting.

▲ A white garden urn holding a moss sphere stoically sits in an old child's ladder-back chair. The similar colors and worn finishes of the chair and urn blend well and draw the eye to the differing color and texture of the moss.

▲ An ironstone dinner plate and single silver candlestick make a spare statement on the fireplace mantel. A collection of river rocks, with their harmonizing shades of tan, white, and gray, add a base of texture and color.

▶ Bird decoys, whether reproduction or antique, have always been a favorite collectible. A working swan decoy, once used in a pond or stream to attract geese, now rests on a blanket chest in the mudroom. The abstract painting hanging over the decoy creates interesting contrast.

A bright blue table stands on the side lawn, with the garden as its backdrop. The Victorian pitchers hold fragrant peonies in soft shades of pink and white. The vibrant punch of color from the primitive table contrasts beautifully with the arrangements it supports and creates a point of focus in the yard.

The whiteness of this room brings the simple lines of these rustic Adirondack chairs into silhouette. They are mainly used on the front porch, but in a pinch, they can easily be moved to the guest bedroom. Softened with blue and white fabric pillows, they entice guests to relax after the long trip to Vermont or enjoy reading a favorite novel.

Using common items in uncommon ways can lead to appealing results. Here, firewood becomes a great backdrop for the bed. Not only is the wood visually interesting, it can be burned in the fireplace. In keeping with the theme, a primitive white fireplace mantel acts as the bed's headboard. A great space for a cozy night's sleep, this room promotes a great sense of peacefulness.

◄ Autumn twigs from the maple tree in the yard add interest to an ordinary grouping of ironstone platters displayed on the wall. Each season can present its own unique display—pussy willows or green moss in spring, favorite garden blooms in summer, or fragrant boughs of balsam during the holidays.

▲ Sheltering such items as flowerpots and a watering can, this distressed commode (an inexpensive yard-sale find) makes a wonderful catchall for the back porch. Even in the winter months, it greets visitors with its unexpected presence out of doors. The white shelf on the wall and the wicker laundry basket (awaiting postal deliveries) complete the roomlike setting.

Chapter 3

Living Among Your Favorite Things

A collection brings together objects that are meaningful to you. Many of the pieces tell a story. They speak to your passions, interests, and perhaps even your history. As your home is a reflection of you, so too are your cherished collections. Live well among your favorite things.

Collecting ironstone has always been a passion. Ironstone pitchers are great by themselves, in groups, or as a way to accent other pieces. You can do more than fill them with flowers: think seasonally, with items such as flags, evergreens, or even tree branches. A votive placed on an upside-down glass in a pitcher will make it glow, creating a soft mood. A group of three or more pitchers used in this way creates a wonderful effect.

Born and raised on a rural Vermont farm, my father lived a life that is best described as simple, and he managed to surround himself with the things that were most important to him. It is the rare picture that doesn't show my father with a cat or a dog, a chicken or a duck, maybe in his arms or sharing a chair—or even perched precariously on his head! My father's gentle spirit spoke clearly through his love for animals and nature. How wonderful that his life could be spent surrounded by the creatures and objects that he loved the most.

Things that we choose to have near us tell the story of our lives. The mementos we deem worthy to be framed on the wall tell the story of where we have been, just as our friends around us every day tell the story of who we are.

I think that larger living spaces offer an opportunity to reflect who you are as a family, while more personal spaces reveal your individuality. By choosing items that bring you personal comfort, you give others insight into who you are. It is wonderful to enter a home alive with children, pets, and family. Your house has captured your essence if the air still rings with those voices and carries a hint of fresh-baked bread long after the children have grown and the bread has been enjoyed. Therefore, decorate your home with the things that bring a smile to your face or take you to another time. Then, like glowing embers on a winter night, the memories will continue to warm you every day of your life.

I choose items carefully and thoughtfully. The true value of a piece cannot accurately be put in monetary terms. Certainly, there are priceless antiques, rare finds, and one-of-a-kinds. But to me, the intrinsic value of a piece goes well beyond what it will bring at the auction block. One such item can be found in a top drawer in our kitchen: my grandmother's ice cream scoop. I can still see my grandmother, elbow-deep in the cold container of freshly made ice cream, filling our bowls one scoop at a time with the rich treat. Homemade ice cream is as much a treat now as when we were growing up, and her scoop is used today just as lovingly as it was half a century ago. In the world of kitchen gadgets, I suspect there are newfangled ice cream scoops that form a perfectly sized ball neatly and quickly every time. But we choose to use my grandmother's ice cream scoop because every time we do, it brings back memories and creates a sense of comfortable tradition as delicious as the ice cream itself.

I believe that the first step in decorating your home should be to choose items that have emotional value. You will find that if an object is important to you, for whatever reason, it will blend into your home design with relative ease. Worry about scale, color, and placement later. That will come much more naturally than you think when you have all the right elements.

I was recently visiting a friend who is an avid collector of vintage toys and memorabilia. When I asked him which toy was his favorite, he looked at me with amazement and replied that they were all his favorites, each and every one. His home was filled from floor to ceiling with interesting and unique items, but he could tell you a story or two about each piece. He knew where it came from, how he found it, and even how much he had paid. He truly adores the objects that surround him.

Most of us do not have the space to display hundreds of our favorite things. We could, however, share a small collection. I have accumulated many ironstone pieces—bowls, pitchers, and platters—each with interesting patterns, patinas, and shades of white. I love them all, for they remind me of our busy kitchen, where lunch and dinner were often prepared at the same time. I have chosen a few of my favorite bowls and pitchers of varying sizes and colors and display them on an open shelf. I also have an array of platters displayed as artwork on the wall. The rest are used every day as intended and grace the dinner table without need for a special occasion.

We can best appreciate design or art when elements of the display resonate within us. Perhaps it is the shape, texture, light, or form of the piece, or perhaps the piece reminds us of someone, someplace, or something. You may not quite be able to determine the reason why an object elicits an emotional response, yet when something appeals to you at a deeper level, it is helpful to take heed. Your response can be the key to living your life and decorating your home in your unique style. Seek these wonderful items out. Use them. If you decorate from the inside out, creative ideas will flow.

My mother loved decorating for the various seasons. She kept decorations for fall, winter, spring, and summer tucked away in the back of the closet until the time came to bring them out. These are things that were important to her—gifts, art we had made as kids, objects that had been passed down. She always found a way to display them for all to see, whether hanging them on the window to catch the light, setting them on the fireplace mantel, or creating artful arrangements on other surfaces. These decorations gave her comfort.

The holiday season is rich with family tradition. The Christmas tree, in particular, can proudly display your favorite things. Each ornament tells a story or sparks a memory, creating a tree as unique as the family that hangs those ornaments on the boughs. Remember the stories these items tell and surround yourself with them. Bring them out where they can be heard, even if only for a few weeks each winter.

There is a long-standing joke about the wonderful apple pies I bake, since I can get lost in sharing the details of how I bake them— perfect crust, apples picked at the right time that are neither too sweet nor too tart. Truth is, it has been a while since I have made an apple pie, but twenty years of reminiscing surely must have preserved my skills! It seems like

yesterday when I picked the apples from the tree behind the house, used my grandmother's butter-stained recipe card to create the perfect flaky crust, and baked the pie in that deep dish that has been around forever.

That experience remains as vivid today as it was twenty years ago. I believe that it is because there was so much more to the experience than looking up a recipe and re-creating a stranger's apple pie. It was indeed personal.

Today more than ever, we understand the connection between our state of mind and our well-being. We know that we are the happiest and healthiest when we nurture our soul. What better way to do that than to surround yourself with things that bring you happiness and comfort! Live well and be well among your favorite things.

► Early children's shoes have always been whimsical collectors' items. The patina of every shoe is different. One wonders who once owned them—were they worn working in the farm's fields or walking a city sidewalk, were they from wealth or poverty? My collection is partly family heirlooms (shoes worn on the farm) and partly shoes collected according to style, condition, and color. Many are orphans, found one at a time. They can be admired individually or placed in a bowl, where they can be admired as a group and moved from place to place to be noticed and loved again.

▲ Early- to mid-nineteenth-century children's shoes spill out of an old distressed child's bureau. Original printed paper still lines the drawers, which may have held similar shoes years ago.

◄ Collecting small items can be great if you have limited space. Butter pats were once found on most dinner tables and used every day. Today these objects, which look like tiny plates, are appreciated for their shape, transfer designs, color, and textures and can be reused in new fun ways. Butter pats look great stacked by themselves, holding a small tea light candle, or serving up name tags for dinner parties. They can even hold butter!

Open your cupboards, drawers, and storage nooks and bring out the meaningful things you find. Enjoy them out in the open again. My grandfather's pocket watches were handed down to my father and then to me and were shuffled around for years. They now have a prominent place in the living room, resting on an old cracked pearlware platter with a blue-feathered edge. They no longer tell the correct time, but I always wonder where they have been in their travels and how many times they were gazed upon for the time of day. They are appreciated today for their shape, wear, and of course, their family history.

Flowerpots come in many shapes and sizes—some with moss growing on them and some with old paint. Grouped together, they can be stunning. At the back door of the farmhouse, sitting on the old table, there is always a stack ready to be filled. Even in the winter months, they are a constant reminder that spring is just around the corner.

The rich copper, orange, and umber hues of a grouping of ordinary terra-cotta flowerpots make an extraordinary visual statement.

Since their inception, flower frogs have been used as utilitarian pieces at the bottom of a flower vase. But they come in wonderful shapes, sizes, and colors and are appreciated and collected today just for that. They can be stacked on a sunroom table as a creative piece of sculpture or used to hold holiday decorations, such as small American flags, on an informal outdoor dining table.

Simple arrangements can make a dramatic statement. Three ironstone
bowls with their pressed scalloped designs, in mottled shades of
white, perhaps with a chip here and there, sit proudly on a primitive
robin's-egg-blue farm cupboard. Together, the bowls and cupboard create
a visual impact. Remember to leave space around each item in such a
display, as it lends the pieces more importance.

Themed displays can be a creative strategy for items that are not part of a larger collection. Sitting on an old whitewashed bureau in the upstairs hall is a beach-themed composition. The watercolor, found at a thrift store in a seaside town in Maine, shares the space with a single starfish. Together, they are just enough to be appreciated but not overwhelming.

▼ A surf-worn seashell rests on a stack of white ironstone platters, creating an enjoyable medley of textures, tones, and curves.

▲ Seashells, bowls, and plates are stacked and piled high. Their beauty is in the simplicity of their whites.

▶ Displaying utilitarian items can be practical as well as beautiful if you have limited storage space. This useful collection of scrub brushes, sponges, and wire cleaning utensils has been taken out of the cupboard and placed on the counter. An attractive old soup tureen that lost its lid long ago serves as their vase. The bowl and platter that frame the tureen provide the finishing touches to this kitchen vignette.

▼ Chairs are not just for sitting. A stack of vintage bowls rests on a primitive child's ladder-back chair. The chair cradles and highlights the bowl collection, yet they remain within easy reach for mixing the next batch of cookies.

▲ Everyday items that must be kept within reach can still be displayed as a collection. Many of my white baking dishes, platters, and bowls are used daily, but when not in use, they are stored in an appealing group on a commercial baker's rack in the kitchen. When purchasing necessary items like these, make a mental note of how they could be arranged at home. Imagine how they would work as a group, perhaps arranged by color or shape.

Since I make collectible teddy bears, there are always two or three bruins, as I like to call them, tucked away somewhere in the house. I like to combine or layer collections together; I not only save space, but I am also able to showcase each piece. I might place the bears in an old wooden chair or in a favorite cupboard, or just rest them in an old child's wagon. Going one step further, I may use a small object, such as a brass sleigh bell tied around a bear's neck, to achieve even more enjoyable layering effects.

▲ Collecting sea glass is a great pastime at the beach. Here, the tiny sea-worn pieces are grouped by their hues of blue and jumbled on an old small platter. The imperfect oil painting of the sea is used as a backdrop, reminding one of the origins of the glass and the long summer days of beachcombing.

◀ Showing off your collections in a subtle way lessens the possibility of visual overload. Leaving the cupboard door open a crack allows you to see the sizable ironstone pitcher collection inside but still to appreciate the primitive pine jelly cupboard. The blue interior of the space separates the shapes and sizes of the ironstone, while the worn area on the cupboard draws your eye back out and lets you focus on the cupboard.

▶ I love Santas and have been making them for years. I always try to keep the first Santa of each of the different series I create. Here, my rag Santa is paired with an old family rag doll. They make quite an unusual, whimsical couple, but they do work well together. And who said Santa always used reindeer? In the farmhouse, these two enjoy a year-round ride on a primitive child's rocking horse.

▲ I have never been one to line books up on a shelf. For a casual cottage look, stack them up on tables, floors, ottomans, or just about anywhere. Books stacked like this create a homey feel for any space. Here in the sunroom, the stacks help me to easily access my favorite read. Stacking them at different heights creates interest as well as improvised pedestals for garden statuary, flower arrangements, or other items one may wish to highlight.

▼ An early bovine print in a gray filigree frame works well with the flea-market-find 1950s Maine license plate. Displaying them on the off-white distressed fireplace mantel reveals this as a collection of tones and textures.

I have gardens full of many varieties of daylilies, and I just love them. However, since they only last for a day, they really don't work well in arrangements with other flowers. For that reason, it was always a challenge to enjoy them inside. After many experiments, I finally found a way of showing off the textures and vibrant colors of these garden beauties. Place a small amount of water in a butter pat and settle your favorite blossom in each. Then arrange them perhaps in a row or a circle on a side table, windowsill, or bathtub ledge. They can serve as the centerpiece at your dining table, or you can place individual blossoms on your desk or in a small nook. Their beauty may be even more touching because it is short-lived.

▲ Little tin spice containers hold the tips of spring lilacs. Such miniature arrangements work well where a pop of color or soft fragrance is needed. Try using other small containers such as teacups or bottles for the same effect.

◄ A doll's blue willow china tea set holds bright green ferns for a splash of spring color.

▲ A French linen slipcovered wing chair keeps company with a folk art Dalmatian. The whites in this welcoming nook, including the walls and the distressed column in the background, all work together.

◀ Collecting folk art is one of my favorite pastimes— and I find it so pleasant to live with. Locally made works supply the theme for the family room. A hand-carved rooster along with the patriotic rag Santa and the distressed primitive dollhouse speak whimsy. When grouped with architectural items, such as the old porch columns, a weathered Palladian window, and the iron acorn finials, the room becomes an eclectic, interesting, and inviting space.

You can never have too many platters. Hang them on the wall, stack them on a shelf, or use them. They are easily found for reasonable prices at tag sales and flea markets. Remember, discoloration, chips, and cracks only add interest and tell the story of their use. These mottled white ironstone platters are grouped by similar shape and size to make an artistic statement.

Every room should have a focal point. This can be achieved by highlighting an object by shape, size, or, as in this room, by color. Subtle shades of white compose the small den, so by setting a worn iron urn filled with white hyacinths on a primitive cupboard, you draw the eye directly to the green leaves. The reflection in the old silvered mirror makes the focus even more dramatic; placing the focal point higher in the room also strengthens the effect.

An early barrel-back cupboard houses a collection of Victorian water pitchers. Grouped by color and shape, the ironstone makes a strong statement, while the cupboard's dark interior highlights the pieces, allowing the viewer to focus on the collection as a whole.

Old glass bottles in soft shades of green, blue, violet, and amber are readily available at flea markets and second-hand stores. They make wonderful vases for single freshly-cut flowers. Here, a grouping of clear bottles holding crisp white bleeding hearts creates a design that is delicate but strong in textures.

Pairing your favorite collectibles with holiday-related items can make for appealing seasonal décor. This mid-1800s child's horse rocker with aging white and red paint works well with the vintage cotton American flags. The flags are being held by a Styrofoam ball covered in moss that rests in the rocker's seat.

Inexpensive and easily found, old dinner plates are a staple for today's cottage decorating ideas. In this array on a fireplace mantel, the seashells claim the foreground and the plates serve as a secondary background.

An assembly of handled and rimmed ironstone harmonizes with the curves of a rusted dark garden urn. As the group rests on the soft, gray blanket box, the colors become familiar with one another. Don't be shy about mixing fine china, iron, and wood together as a collection of your favorite things.

Chapter 4

Working with Nature

Mother Nature embraces you wherever you go; in return, embrace her in your home. Let her take part in your decorating, whether through cut flowers from the garden or the display of an abandoned bird's nest. Harmonizing with nature creates harmony in your home.

Having a stately architectural element in a garden can be an effective way to draw attention to a special area. A pine arbor off the side of the farmhouse is the gateway to a secluded garden. The latticed side panels corral the overabundance of mature perennials in the height of summer. Looking through the arbor, one sees a perfectly framed picture of the back garden and the large pond in the distance.

For years our ancestors fought to carve out the space needed for farming. Cornfields, hayfields, gardens, all were wrested from Mother Nature herself. But she would patiently lie in wait for the year the garden soil would go unturned or the hayfield would be left standing, and then she would creep in and retake what we knew was hers all along. Our claim to the land has always been a temporary agreement sealed with the sweat of countless hours cutting, digging, and hacking away. It speaks to her gentle and steadfast character that Mother Nature can undo the work of men so quietly and effortlessly.

Working against nature is exhausting, endless work. While we sleep, she does not. Working with nature is an entirely different experience. Working with nature involves give and take, compromise, and an understanding of your place in the scheme. Consult with Mother Nature in your design efforts. In the end, you will enjoy outcomes that far exceed anything you could have created on your own. You both will revel in this symbiotic relationship and know that you have been part of something unique and beautiful.

A stone wall emerges from the dense undergrowth and towering pine trees and stretches forever both in time and distance. The forest it now encircles was once the tilled field from whence the stones were unearthed. It seems impossible that each of these stones was wrenched from the soil to build this grand wall. This is an example of the work achieved when forces are joined. The earth will give as many stones as are needed, and man will give as many hours as he must. The resulting work of art adorns fields and forests like a string of pearls. If Mother Nature is happy with the wall, it will last.

Consider also the woodpile. Anyone who has attempted to stack a cord of firewood in a straight, freestanding row knows that there is more to the task than meets the eye. It will lean, it will sag, it will wind up on the ground unless there is an understanding that Mother Nature has assigned each piece its place. Taking the time to build the puzzle thoughtfully is a better investment than rushing, toppling the pile, and having to begin again.

The placement of shrubs, perennials, and ponds, even of roads and homes, needs to be carefully planned and considered. Unilateral decisions made without Mother Nature's input will ultimately cost time and money. A few years ago, we planted a row of hemlocks to give privacy to our yard. We knew that one end of the hedgerow was windy while the other more protected, but we figured that with care, we could overcome that. Of course, the result was disheartening. Today, one end of the row has been replaced with cedar, while the other end is thriving hemlock. Had we consulted with nature during the planning phase, we would have saved ourselves a lot of money, time, and work.

Many years ago, a dear friend, mentor, and avid perennial gardener gave me advice I have only recently come to appreciate and understand: "If your plants aren't happy, move them to where they will be happy, and they will care for themselves," she said. Well, I spent several years trying to make some plants happy where they just did not fit in before I began to realize her message. Shade plants need the shade; sun worshippers need the sun. Some like their feet wet, others prefer dry. Keep an eye on new plants—some will argue with their neighbors, some will demand more space. Others will reward you and thrive almost regardless of their surroundings. If you have plants in your garden that attract deer, don't be surprised to find the creatures there. If they aren't welcome, then reconsider your plant selection and maybe add a bit of fencing!

When your plants are happy and healthy, you will also notice that the color scheme and variety seem to work on their own. Mother Nature is, of course, a master gardener. Healthy plants need little care. If they are placed where they get what they need from the environment, your responsibility to them is lessened.

Working with nature presents the same rewards and challenges inside your home. Color, texture, height, and form all come into play when considering placement and containers for plants or cut flowers. Cut flowers will tell you which container they need to be in; potted plants will let you know if they need more foot room. Most of us probably spend as much time admiring our gardens through a window from inside as standing outside among the plants. Design the plantings so that you are rewarded equally from inside or out.

Here in Vermont, we are fortunate to live in an area so rich in natural beauty. Behind our home stands Salt Ash Mountain. There, we first see the brilliant greens of spring; the lush dark hues of summer; the brilliant reds, yellows, and oranges of autumn; and the whites of early winter. The mountain is an ever-changing backdrop of color, a harbinger of the days to come, and a steadfast companion. Considering the natural beauty of your surroundings is an important step in creating the design of your environment. Plan your garden with several layers in mind. What does your eye see first, then next? What is the backdrop for your garden? If you lack a natural backdrop, can you create one that works in your space? Take the time to listen and you may discover that a hedge, taller plants, or perhaps a fence or stone wall is just what your garden is asking for.

Clay terra-cotta flowerpots, old watering cans, and a bee skep rest on a low stone wall, waiting for their next creative use in the garden. They are visually pleasing, even when idle, and can be admired for their lack of organization.

A patch of asparagus will return each year in the same spot it was lovingly planted perhaps a century ago. The swallows insist on nesting in the eaves of the barn each year to raise another brood. The woodcock in the meadow does the same high twirling dance on warm spring nights. A doe and fawn find shelter from the midday sun in the stand of maples behind the pond. A weary gardener retires to a rocking chair on the porch. In working with nature, we have become a part of the whole.

Whatever their placement, perennial alliums command center stage. The bright purple flowers with feathery edges belong to the onion family and are favorites in early spring gardens. Alliums come in many varieties to suit any garden, from those with huge round blossoms as big as a cantaloupe, to shorter, more petite types that bloom at different times throughout the summer season.

Old tin watering cans that no longer hold water can still be used in your garden; they make great outdoor art. Here, several are placed strategically in a patch of fragrant lavender. They also can be used as flowerpots in your garden, patio, or outdoor sitting area.

Freshly picked daffodils are clumped together in an ironstone milk pitcher. Resting on the seat of an early child's ladder-back chair, the arrangement is showcased in an unusual manner to be enjoyed by both young and old.

Spring gardens delight everyone with the first blossoms of the year. Mixing early spring bulbs with later-blooming perennials will reward you with the earliest possible arrival of color to the winter-drab flowerbeds. Here, coral bells mingle with violas, creating a sprinkling of color among the soon-to-be-blooming iris. Removing old blossoms from the stems encourages new blooms to appear before the plant's flowering season is over.

◀ A plain ironstone platter with an impressed rim holds a delicately edged woodland fern. The harmony of the shapes and the image of the feather-light plant resting on the heavy ironstone make for a dramatic, but unfussy, display. Plate arrangements like this work well in areas where space is limited and height is not needed, for instance on a side table or windowsill.

▲ Anyone who has taken a woodland walk knows that many varieties of wild ferns grow in the forest. Delicate in form and rich in their varying shades of green, these plants work wonders as interior decorating details. Here, the word fern spelled out with individual fronds makes a whimsical and creative centerpiece for the casual dining room table.

◀A hedge of triple apricot daylilies, mixed in with other perennials, welcomes all who come to the farmhouse's front porch. The individual blossoms are fleeting, but the floral display lasts for weeks, thanks to the many buds that open daily. A foolproof perennial that is practically disease-free and content to stay within its boundaries, the daylily is truly a favorite in the garden.

▶Foxgloves have been garden favorites for centuries. Most are biannual and are renewed by dropped seeds from the original plants. Therefore, in order for the seed to germinate and grow, they should not be mulched. Here, a perennial variety of yellow foxglove is displayed in a silver water pitcher. This variety will come back year after year and make a stunning cut-flower arrangement.

◀A pair of garden wellies stands on the porch overlooking the cement rooster in the flowerbeds below. These rubber boots are a must for the gardener; they keep feet dry and can be left at the door so the mud stays outside.

▼ Mahogany bee balm stands guard at the front door of the studio, waiting to be admired by the next passerby. Gardens should be enjoyed from the inside just as much as from the outside, especially on rainy and chilly days.

▲ An old church pew is given new life in the garden. Weatherproofed with bright white marine paint, the bench now sits on the banks of the pond, flanked by two hand-sculpted Canadian hemlock trees. Garden benches can be fashioned from all sorts of objects, so find the one that is comfortable and visually appropriate for your special space.

◄ Silver king artemisia shimmers among the darker shades of greens. A showy leaf perennial, artemisia seems to spread by dancing through the other established plantings.

▶ It is important to reap the hard work of gardening by enjoying the color and scents you have brought forth—and nothing is more comforting than doing this from the vantage of a porch rocker in midsummer. The front farmhouse garden offers showy flowers ranging from white gooseneck loosestrife and tall, fragrant garden phlox to frilly bee balm and yellow coreopsis.

◀Freshly picked daylilies make a colorful, fragrant plate arrangement. The brightly colored, short-lived blooms sing like a choir on an ironstone platter. Combined with the bright blue striped tablecloth, this palette will brighten up any area, inside or out.

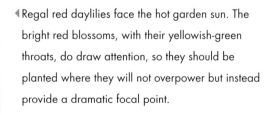

◀Old-fashioned yellow daylilies are a sunny sight. These beauties are known for their peppery fragrance and can be seen in the garden from afar.

◀Regal red daylilies face the hot garden sun. The bright red blossoms, with their yellowish-green throats, do draw attention, so they should be planted where they will not overpower but instead provide a dramatic focal point.

Nothing brightens the late-spring garden better than lilacs. They come in many varieties, from trees to bushes, from early bloomers to late. The double whites shown here are among my favorites. Rich in texture and fragrance, these beauties will last up to a week in fresh water. They are the perfect scented visual for any dining room table, bedside stand, or busy office.

Having limited space in your house can be a challenge. One solution is to seek maximum impact from small-scale objects. Here, a small English transferware teacup holds a tiny sprig of dark purple lilac. This yard sale find is now a prized vase for this fragrant bouquet. Anything that will hold water can become a vase, so use your imagination.

An embossed pitcher holds a handful of freshly picked lilacs. The mottled whites and imperfections of the pitcher echo the dainty petals of the colorful lilacs. Placed on a table by a lamp, it enhances the sitting area and invites all to enjoy.

Using garden statuary or art in the farmhouse garden is a great way to bring more texture to your space. Iron is always a good choice for garden statuary or art. It has a strong presence and contributes texture; the harsh elements only improve its patina. This sundial sits in the middle of a round garden at the back of the farmhouse. Not only do its shape and height work well in this spot, it also offers the weary gardener the afternoon time.

The sound of trickling water in the garden is so calming. On this cement fountain, three cherubs hold an umbrella as protection against the falling water. Birds love it and use it frequently for bathing and drinking. Replace the water every few days to make sure it is fresh, and avoid using chemicals so it is safe for wildlife.

A rustic twig set, consisting of a settee, two chairs, and a coffee table, welcomes you to the back garden and provides you with an outdoor living room with pond views. This set is made of naturally weather-resistant red cedar. Building a fire in the terra-cotta chimney takes the chill off during the early evenings and creates flames to gaze upon without heating the house.

◀ A walk down a dirt road in the country, especially during early fall, is always a delight. Here, Rooster, our golden retriever, takes his daily walk to the neighbors' house for a quick treat or new toy to be brought back home.

▶ Freshly picked hydrangeas fill a rusted iron urn on the kitchen worktable. Garden pumpkins and gourds surround its base to create the perfect fall scene. Hydrangeas can also easily be dried: Cut them before the first frost and hang them upside down in a dark space. After this treatment, they hold up well and can even be sprayed with color when they start to fade.

◄ Green and yellow decorative gourds huddle in a worn silver-plate bowl. Freshly fallen leaves scooped up from outside and placed around its base complete this organic fall centerpiece. This easy, elegant arrangement will last for weeks.

▲ Brightly colored Indian corn rests on an apple green jelly cupboard. The distressed gold-leaf mirror adds shimmering golden hues to the composition. This low-key fall arrangement will attract the eyes of many and will last from the early fall through to the Thanksgiving holiday.

▶ Sitting in the sleeping daylily garden are two white French bistro chairs. Now only perches for the blue jays and chickadees, they add linear detail to the winter landscape. The folk art bird feeder, perched upon a copper pedestal, was made by a local artisan and attracts many varieties of birds throughout the winter months.

▼ A vintage German watering can sits on the table just outside the back porch door. At rest for the winter season, it adds interest to a rather subdued scene. Leaving a few chosen items out can draw attention to the different areas out of doors.

▲ The rustic twig furniture is now a resting place for the first snow of winter. The antique birdbath has begun its wait for warmer days. This summer gathering place becomes a visual focal point when all else in the garden is covered in white.

Earlier in the season, snow completely blanketed these single-plank-backed Adirondack lawn chairs. Since then, though, sun-filled days have melted the deep snow so that it could settle. The chairs now peek through the heavy, wet covering, showing their form and distressed white paint again.

Making your own wooden architectural garden pieces allows you to create exactly the look you want while also being cost-effective. Here, a wooden pedestal, built to match the Greek revival trim on the farmhouse, stands like a soldier at the foot of the driveway. A reproduction cement acorn finial completes the piece.

Terra-cotta pots, some with chipped paint and others bearing a hint of a mossy exterior, are jumbled on the back porch shelf, accompanied by a wicker basket. They rest, knowing their purpose will resume with the coming of spring.

Chapter 5

Embracing the Qualities of Color

You can just feel it when the colors are right. Achieving a sense of comfort through the use of color is pure magic. With attention to light, contrast, background, and intention, you can make your home shine.

Grouping items by color is a stunning way to create a display. These stacks of early yellowware mixing bowls display the same rich golden and toasted hues as the handmade mohair teddy bear. The weathered bruin, with his back-supporting collection of bowls, brings a welcome touch of whimsy to the kitchen, either on a worktable or countertop.

I believe that the interpretation of color, like an interpretation of music or the subtle bouquet of a glass of fine wine, is as individual as each one of us. I also believe that life experience and the environment in which one was raised shape the experience of color. My own impressions of color are largely drawn from my roots in New England. New Englanders' lives change with the seasons, and we associate certain colors with certain climates and kinds of comfort. Because of our environment, perhaps, we experience colors differently from those living in areas less affected by changing seasons. In Vermont, each year starts with a new, fresh canvas of white. On the brightest day, our sun reflects in the snow crystals, giving the impression of a cool blue blanket. It is from our experience, then, that certain shades of blue have a fresh, crisp winter-day quality. As the seasons change our senses are challenged to adjust to the transition from winter's white canvas to spring's vibrancy to the lush tones of summer and finally to the brilliant hues of autumn. Then, like the artist that she is, Mother Nature signs her work and starts anew with a canvas of white.

The quintessential New England village mimics nature's canvas in the clean, white clapboards of traditional homes and churches. The red barn, too, reflects a color found in each of our seasons, from apple blossoms and bee balm in spring and summer, to autumn maples and winter berries. Dark greens are present all year as well, as are the neutral tans and off-whites. The environment has given permission for these colors, and they will always work. Pay attention to your surroundings. Nature will offer you a palette of colors you can trust.

As New Englanders, we have come to associate color with season and season with climate. We experience blue as a cool color, as it reflects in winter's snow. The darker, more lush shades of green, mustard, and red are associated with the heat of summer; thus when we bring them into our homes, we also bring their warmth. The brighter colors of autumn hint of crisp nights, so it is no wonder that the harvest colors of orange and yellow leave us sensing a frost may be in the air. Each of these colors possesses different qualities, each holds a unique energy, and each should be used thoughtfully in your decorating.

When we completed the renovation of our home, we discovered that we had completely changed the interior by inviting in so much of the outside world. The vivid gardens became a large part of our interior color scheme as we welcomed them in through numerous French doors and new windows. Suddenly, the colors of the seasons became a part of our interior. I went back to my days of painting, where each new work began as a clean canvas. That experience of adding layers of color to the blank foundation became my inspiration, and I began to create an interior of white and shades of white. Floors, walls, and even the ceiling became the canvas for nature's colorful strokes. As the light of each day changes a bit with the seasons and the gardens mature and evolve throughout the year, the interior of our home changes in response.

Whether inside your home or outside in the garden, it is fun to experiment with color. Some colors produce a dramatic effect when grouped together in similar but subtly varying shades. It can also be fun to work with the unexpected contrast of colors, textures, or forms. I often use ironstone, pewter, or glass for cut flowers and enjoy the effect as nature's colors dance for attention. I think this explains my fondness for old painted furniture as well. Looking at the several layers of paint on a piece, I find the pattern formed by the various textures and contrasting colors peeking through the cracks to be unique. Place these items as carefully in your home as you would a colorful floral arrangement and enjoy the effect.

Qualities of color are never more evident than during winter's bright white days. It is a time of reflective light and vibrant color. Snow crystals reflect the sun and moon and create the brightest days and nights of the year. Winterberries and evergreens stand out boldly against the snowy landscape, while at the feeder, the cardinal and blue jay make their dazzling presence known. Winter is the potential and promise of Mother Nature's new canvas for the year. Soon enough, spring colors will be introduced. Colors will begin to melt into one another, warming the canvas, and once again, we will find ourselves standing in her masterpiece.

White, one of the most widely used colors in decorating, is neither plain nor simple; it is available in a multitude of shades and tones. Here in the farmhouse den, a primitive cream-colored jelly cupboard catches direct light from the afternoon sun. Antique mirrors with white frames and the luminous ironstone pitcher layer on more tones. Add these to the white walls, floor, and canvas-covered chair, and the room becomes one, even though the white shades are different and appreciated differently.

When we painted this jelly cupboard, we made it look old and weathered by using a dry-brush technique and gave it a bright contrasting robin's egg blue interior that's ideal for highlighting the ironstone collection. Playing colors against one another adds depth and interest to rooms and painted furniture.

Drapes in vibrant shades of orange, pink, and white serve as a backdrop for the similarly colored daylilies on the side table in front of the window. The colors make the area bright and cheery, just perfect for a summer's day.

◀Crisp white roses in a small pitcher add a touch of elegance to any area. The green leaves and stems look more vibrant against the soft whites of the roses, pitcher, and table.

◀A paint's finish—glossy, satin, flat, or eggshell—changes the quality of the color it projects. Here, the farm table is painted with a high-gloss, oil-based enamel paint, which is durable and washable. It is paired with a group of ladder-back chairs painted in the same shade of white but with a flat finish. The way the light reflects off these objects makes them appear different in color. As a result, the set has more of a mix-and-match or as-found feel.

⬈ You can use contrast to make a color pop in a monochrome setting. In a guest bedroom at the farmhouse, black-and-white toile fabric covers a comfy chaise longue. The white in the toile blends with the color of the ironstone, as well as that of the doll's dress—so the black in the toile stands out spectacularly.

⬈ Green gourds are paired with a vintage blue canning jar to produce an artistic effect.

◄ Using a clear-glass container as a vase makes the color of the flowers in it appear more intense. Vibrant purple coneflowers from the garden seem almost to be standing on their own when placed in this vase.

► A group of similar pieces displayed together can have a greater impact than they would individually, especially when contrasting color is used. English pewter water pitchers lining the mantel overflow with green limelight hydrangeas. The muted shades of the pewter allow the contrasting color of the hydrangeas to make a bold statement in the room.

▶ The small size of these pillows allows many of them to be used on this canvas-covered sofa in the sunroom without consuming it. The sofa's lines and shape can still be appreciated, while the royal blue of the repeating stripes adds vibrancy.

▲ Bright yellow flowers, like these daisies, are a quick and easy way to add color and warmth to any room that needs a little cheer.

▲ Bring everyday items out of the closets and drawers and show off their colors while they wait to be used. Layers of tattletale gray Turkish towels rest on a scrubbed European folding chair in the bathroom. The off-whites, soft grays, and light blues of the towels harmonize with one another and with the pine chair.

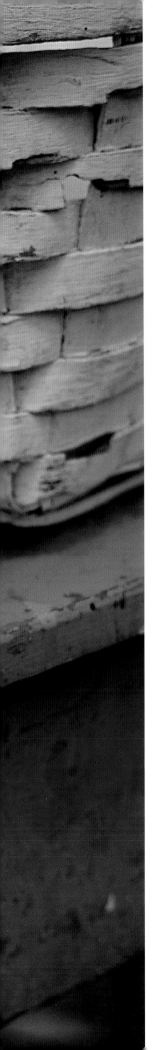

◄Freshly cut peonies rest on a painted farm table. The contrast of the pink against the cheery blue adds interest to both colors. This color strategy works well with accessories but is not recommended for large areas, such as walls or large furniture. In those instances, colors that belong to the same family should be used.

▶Objects that reflect light and display appealing colors will liven up any dark space in your home. A yellowy-green framed mirror leans against the wall, a backdrop for a pairing of similarly toned but different collectibles. The scratched enameled-tin plate mimics the crackled silver mirror both in finish and luminosity. The antique green glass bottle mimics the frame's color, and the Queen Anne's lace it holds completes the vignette.

◄Similar colors work well together in large spaces as well as small. These stoneware crocks in creamy glazes make congenial companions for the brown earthenware pitcher, which, in turn, draws attention to the rich brown of the crocks' interiors. The splint basket's warm tone adds to the harmony of the grouping.

▲ A cracked and stained ironstone pitcher would be considered a throwaway by many. But here, its varied tones complement the gray chipped paint of the wooden finial. The crooked lines of the dark brown twigs add further visual interest.

▶ The symmetry of the worn architectural columns in the den showcases the seasonal display between them. The fresh American flag provides a welcome splash of vibrant color, and its wrinkled fabric contributes another texture to the display.

Soft afternoon light pours into a quiet bedroom. The finely stitched blue toile coverlet stands out as the only color in the room. Light and airy, the room's soothing color scheme beckons one in for an afternoon nap.

▶ Brilliant light from several French doors fills the farmhouse living room. A down-filled sofa with a white denim slipcover is positioned in the center of the room. Since only minimal color is used in the room, specifically in the blue striped pillow and checkered barrel chair, those welcoming items of furniture stand out, offering comfort without being overwhelming.

◀ Dark purple lilacs overflow from a pitcher resting on a bold-blue-striped table runner in the dining room. The impact of the two vibrant colors and the sheen of both the pitcher and the platters on the wall make this dining room area fresh and summery.

Chapter 6

Getting a Feel for Texture

Texture, whether in the mottled leaves of a boxwood hedge or the scratches on a well-used wooden bowl, is all around us. Like the pairing of wall and trim colors, texture can help express your personality and make your home all yours.

Stacks of ironstone plates serve as a work of utilitarian art in the farmhouse kitchen. We appreciate them for their crackled glaze, chipped edges, and unevenness, their mosaic of mottled tans, creams, and grays. An ironstone pitcher tops the mountain of china, ready for its next use on the dining table or as a vase for a garden flower arrangement.

A dear friend who was finding new homes for some of her cherished possessions gave me a crazy quilt. It has now become one of my cherished possessions, reminding me of my friend and the times we have shared. It is also a remarkable piece of folk art. Remarkable craftsmanship and labor went into this piece. It can hang as artwork on the wall or offer warmth on a chilly night. Its colors and patterns evoke the image of a perennial garden. But it is the texture that I find most intriguing, that separates it from any other quilt ever created. There is the texture you can see—and then there is the texture you have to experience with your hands. The way the small squares work together and play off one another is masterful. Texture, color, pattern—all speak to the artistic talents and loving hands that created this piece of art.

Each scrap used for the quilt was most likely chosen for a variety of reasons, but today we can only speculate. One may have been from a child's first coat, one from a dress worn on a particularly memorable summer evening. Perhaps there is a baby blanket, work shirt, drape, or tablecloth sewn into it. Perhaps these pieces were chosen for their color, perhaps for their texture, or maybe they were selected for the memory each sparked. Most likely, they were selected for all of these reasons.

I often think of that quilt when working on a project in the house or garden. To be attractive, interesting, and meaningful, the design of a room, a table setting, an arrangement of flowers from the garden, even my choice of attire for a night out must include the elements of color, texture, and pattern, just like that patchwork quilt.

I like to incorporate lots of texture into my designs. Indoors, this might mean grouping furniture with chipped paint with the smooth surfaces of ironstone or pewter or placing a rough stone surface next to smooth, well-worn pine. In the garden, the opportunities for expression through texture are infinite. Picture feathery leaves against woody stalks, or stone against soft moss. Cement statuary, water features, iron, terra-cotta, and brick are other examples of materials that add texture. Color, texture, and form are everywhere, begging to be creatively stitched into a patchwork.

I find that I can trust nature to provide the best elements with which to create, and that natural elements work well in combination with one another. Stone, in its many forms—such as marble, fieldstone, granite, slate, soapstone—offers visual interest as well as functionality for countertops, mantels, flooring, and fireplaces. Wood is another favorite.

Painted, stained, natural, hardwood, or softwood, each type contributes a unique texture. Metals, glass, and fabrics also serve to accentuate and enhance the qualities of one another.

Plants and cut flowers provide a natural texture and quality unlike anything manmade. The graceful bloom of a lily displayed alongside the dull finish of old pewter sets each apart in its uniqueness. The wispy green fern planted in an iron urn highlights contrasts: living and inert, warm and cool, whimsical and austere. Contrast creates definition, focus, and awareness.

The view from atop Salt Ash Mountain is a patchwork of forest, fields of corn, green meadows of hay, and dotted homesteads. Streams, stone walls, and hedgerows stitch the patches together. Each small square is rich in texture; it works with and plays off the other squares masterfully. The inspiration for design is always here for us.

These homespun linen curtains with their nubbly surface contrast with the creamy smooth finish of the ironstone pitcher. Together, they welcome a cool summer breeze.

The impact of patinas and textures is enhanced when objects are combined creatively. Here, a rusty white urn is planted with spring hyacinths in full bloom. An old wavy glass mirror placed behind the urn reflects not only the container's rust-pitted surface but also the smooth leaves and blooms of the plant, magnifying the presence of the floral display in the room.

Speckles of green and umber dance across these decorative gourds in seeming imitation of the equally speckled ironstone platter. This grouping makes a textural statement while showcasing natural, relaxed tones.

A casually stored teapot and plates in the farmhouse pantry displays shades of creamy white and curves against the similarly toned, vertically lined, wainscot background.

A stack of disparate dull-finish pewter vessels creates an unusual centerpiece. Filled with soft blue cornflowers, a roadside weed, the English water pitcher at the top provides the perfect combination of soft textures and colors. Pewter can be left outside for long periods of time, as nature's elements will only add to its patina.

Layers of cracked, chipped paint on this old paneled door speak of generations of use. Pink, green, and white contrast against the natural wood, the years they represent blending into one combined patina. A loosely made twig wreath adds even more texture to the aged door.

The word *antique* frequently brings to mind a family heirloom. These baby shoes—each having lost its mate—pay homage to the eight children who once wore them. Lined up on a weathered sage-green shelf, they are given prominence on the wall, an appealing jumble of shapes, sizes, and degrees of wear.

Hundreds of tiny baby's breath blossoms and buds hover in a soft cloud over the white bowl that holds this cheery arrangement.

This florist variety of green moss has been cleaned and treated to stay green, then molded over Styrofoam balls. Placed atop weathered iron urns, the spheres have the look and texture of growing topiaries, but they need neither pruning nor water. Such carefree topiaries are useful in areas where the sun cannot reach and live plants would struggle.

Rows of antique medicine bottles line this fireplace mantel. The shiny bottles' glow comes from a mini set of white Christmas lights carefully placed behind them. The smooth textures are brightened by the dim lights and the illuminated glass projects soft warmth into the room.

Strong stripes work well with distressed walls and weathered furniture. Resting here by a sunny window, a French reading chair is upholstered with a subtle taupe-and-white herringbone fabric. The smooth fabric sitting next to the weathered bureau, with its multiple layers of peeling paint, makes for an arresting contrast.

This subtle display demonstrates the power of combining many shades and textures of white. The paint on the farmhouse mantel tells its story of age. Adding to the array are the rustic beeswax candles, a variety of ironstone water pitchers, and an antique picture frame.

A silver-plated trophy cup, honoring a long-ago accomplishment, holds a single small American flag, wrinkled yet still vibrant. The dull finish of the tarnished metal and the texture of the cotton flag make an interesting and unexpected juxtaposition.

These early checkerboards tell the story of their long lives through the patterns of wear in the paint. They are sought after today for their fascinating patinas, and for the beauty of the unique grain and color of the wood they are made from. Similar primitive objects, such as painted wall cupboards, tables, and chairs, are also highly collectible.

An eighteenth-century American step-back cupboard in early salmon-colored paint stands proudly in the farmhouse living room. This handy antique, as useful as ever, displays an early wooden trencher from my grandmother's pantry. The softly rubbed patina of the cupboard and the rigid texture of the trencher display well together, as if they have always been in each other's presence.

An ornate silver serving tray, tarnished to a dull, dark gray, presents freshly cut peony blossoms from the garden.

This welcoming foyer surprises everyone who enters it. Hand-painted cedar trees line walls and mimic the live trees just outside the front door. The repeating patterns in the flame-stitch fabric on the sofa pick up the similar hues on the wall, making this a well-balanced room with incredible graphics and textures.

Eyebrow windows in the second-story bedroom illuminate the painted wide-plank floors, exposing their wear and wide cracks. The high-gloss white paint reflects light as if the floor were a mirror. The newly painted reproduction chair with blue-and-white ticking sits between the windows in complete balance.

Made by a neighbor from fresh garden lamb's ear, now dried, preserving the wonderfully soft grayish-white leaves, this wreath hangs against a tin-paneled pie safe. The tiny punched holes that make the design in each piece of tin are softened by the texture of this everlasting ornament.

A long-owned collection of pewter finds a home in a primitive jelly cupboard, which serves as both a display cabinet and a storage place. The textures and colors of the tarnished metal and the unexpected wash of paint inside the cabinet door interact and enhance each other. When a change of look is desired, close the door to bring attention to the cupboard itself.

▲ This early black-and-white print has actually gained appeal and interest since
the water damage it sustained overlaid another dimension on the delicate lines
of the image. The original dark frame has been softened with a light spray of
silver paint, which provides subtle contrast.

▶ The all-white center hall in the farmhouse has doors on each end. Lit with a soft
light in any weather, at any time of day, the room always glows. Keeping the
same or similar colors in a small, busy area such as this and using texture, like
the rough plastered walls and glossy-painted floors, opens up the area as you
walk through.

Chapter 7

Living as if Every Day Were Christmas

Carefully chosen holiday treasures say something about how you want to live each day and help to build delicious holiday anticipation. Wonderful Santas, glowing pumpkins, scary ghosts, and cheery Easter bunnies bring a smile each time they are retrieved from storage for annual display. If they have a place in your heart, they should have a place in your home.

A wreath made from white pine, balsam, and Scotch pine hangs on the plank door at the back porch. The hand-painted whimsical sign, bearing words from a favorite Christmas carol, welcomes all who enter. You can make your own by painting a favorite holiday verse on an interesting piece of weathered or painted wood.

Christmas has always been my favorite time of year. It is the only time I can get away with pulling out all the stops and decorate to my heart's content. I love pulling the special decorations from their hiding places and filling the house with their charm. I suppose they are made more special by the restraint we show in packing them away after the holidays have passed—but if it were up to me, we would keep our treasures out year-round and let the house revel in the holiday spirit through all the seasons.

Winter white is a perfect backdrop for this season. Evergreen boughs, trees, wreaths, and garlands brighten rooms with natural beauty and the fresh scent of the forest. Architectural elements such as mantels or stair railings are traditional locations for holiday décor, but it is the unexpected touches that please me the most. The rocking horse that lives in the corner all year long can be magically transformed into a reindeer when Santa is settled comfortably into his saddle. The baskets in the kitchen can be filled with fragrant greens. The mirror in the hall now frames a fresh wreath of holly, and the iron urn from the garden holds a profusion of green boughs and bright red berries.

On the Christmas trees of my childhood, each bough was adorned with at least one precious decoration. Brightly colored bulbs and tinsel filled the gaps where ornaments could not be secured. If there was space left, our job was not quite done. So it was not until a few years ago that I discovered the beauty of a minimally decorated evergreen tree. A few white lights are draped on the boughs so that its natural beauty can still be enjoyed. The tree stands as it would in the forest after a dusting of snow has fallen on the boughs. The cherished ornaments that once cluttered the tree can now be used elsewhere in the house as colorful accents. I display them in a bowl or place them where their burst of color will be most appreciated.

Each of us brings a bit of our family tradition to the holiday. Traditions are the heart and soul of this season. It may be the one day of the year that Great-grandmother's turkey platter is laden with delicacies or the only time the delicate china is unpacked, admired, and used. Rich family traditions shape who we are today just as we are shaping the traditions of future generations when we explain to a small child how a particular ornament made it into the family or what to look for in choosing the perfect Christmas tree. Revel in traditions and create your own, so that the holiday season is always exciting and new.

Handmade teddy bears lounge in pairs, enjoying the fragrant Christmas tree. The whiteness of the living room, from the hand-hewn beams to the high-gloss pine floors, intensifies the color of the evergreen decorations, as well as of the American-style red and blue bears.

◀ Antique baby shoes, beloved decorations all year, become Christmas tree ornaments during the holiday season. They hang on the small tree in the mudroom, held upright in an old stoneware crock under the supervision of a trio of handmade teddy bears.

▶ This holiday creation is a paper-faced folk-art Santa, reminiscent of the cotton-batting Santa ornaments of the turn of the twentieth century. Made from antique parade bunting, this Santa hangs year-round on the primitive tin-paneled pie safe in the dining room. His off-white beard and trim are fashioned out of cotton batting from frayed quilts too worn to be used as bedding.

◀ A grouping of chalkware Santas stand in front of a mirror, which doubles the apparent size of the crowd. The vibrant Americana stockings, made from old parade bunting and trimmed with vintage tinsel, supply added color and whimsical holiday charm.

▼ After sculpting these Santas out of clay, I made rubber molds to reproduce them in papier-mâché. Reminiscent of German belznickels, each is painted in nonholiday colors and no two are alike. Antique German mica flakes applied to the base resemble snowflakes.

The farm's old woodshed is now a family room and the hub for holiday gatherings. The two striped camelback sofas face an antique tavern table in the center of the room. A balsam Christmas tree stands in the corner, decorated only in Italian lights, so it can be appreciated for its natural beauty. Handmade Santas, swans, and a rocking horse wearing a wreath add whimsy to this holiday setting.

A handmade chalkware Santa cast in an antique German chocolate mold stands in an ironstone bowl. Brushed lightly with silver paint, the Santa resembles an old glass ornament that has discolored over the years. The finishing touch is the glimmering wreath of icy, crystal-like beads.

A freshly cut balsam is cradled by an antique wheelbarrow ready to be brought to the farmhouse for the Christmas holiday.

▶Combining nontraditional and traditional holiday decorations adds to the creativity of this festive season. A dense wreath made from woodland princess pine hangs on the farmhouse wall over an English ironstone tea set. Budding amaryllis are planted in ironstone soup tureens and a mug.

▼Fresh greens are a staple at Christmas. An aromatic cedar garland clings like skirting to the edge of a white pedestal table, a spirited holiday touch in the white living room.

◢A handmade bear, with old button eyes and an old sleigh bell around its neck, sits on the newel post in the center hall. Settled on top of a garland of mixed greens entwining the handrail, the bear catches the eye of anyone who passes. Perhaps his bell is from Santa's sleigh.

A row of budding paperwhites, enticed to open just in time for the holiday season, line the old store counter now used as a serving buffet in the dining room. The bulbs are planted in ironstone bowls and a coverless soup tureen, and the soil has been covered with fresh cranberries to add festive red to the setting.

Clear glass beads are strung on wire hand-shaped to spell the word *peace*. Adorned with green ribbon, the decoration is framed on a pie plate with a blue edge, although of course it could also be hung from a wreath, in a window, or on the Christmas tree. Any holiday greeting can be written this way, and different colored beads will create different looks.

You might never guess that this intricate wreath is made of macaroni. It was found at a local flea market for fifty cents and given its refreshed, gleaming look by being sprayed with chrome paint from the hardware store.

This handmade papier-mâché Santa, bedecked in a nontraditional brown coat with fur trim and with a beard made from old quilt batting, remains on display year-round. His stern expression is reminiscent of early German Santas.

An ocean shell found last summer now becomes part of the holiday décor at the farmhouse. With its pale pink interior and off-white exterior, the shell matches the vintage glass ornaments it holds.

◀ A silver-plated champagne cooler, found at a yard sale, holds a group of frosted aqua blue ornaments, also yard-sale finds. Glass garlands entangle at its fluted base, adding color and holiday cheer.

▲ The early apple green chimney cupboard is the perfect festive color for this handmade chalkware Santa collection. Painted silver to mimic mercury glass, their different shapes and heights create visual interest and reveal the individuality of each piece.

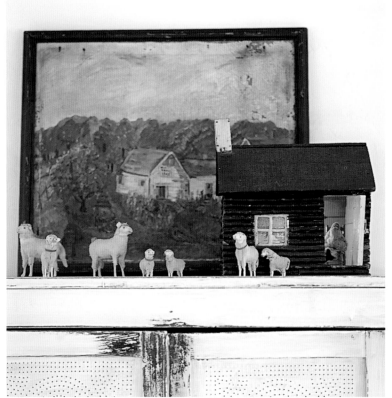

▲ This primitive holiday grouping tells a story. The naive painting in the background sets the backdrop for this cupboard-top display. In the foreground, the lighted Adirondack cabin, with Santa sitting inside and antique Putz sheep grazing outside, sets a pastoral scene.

An antique salmon-painted box holds a collection of vintage glass ornaments. Picked up one at a time at shops, flea markets, and yard sales, they make a cheerful group. Ornaments intended to adorn Christmas trees can be used and displayed in such a multitude of ways. Try tying one onto a special Christmas present in lieu of the traditional bow.

American flags are displayed year-round at the farmhouse and admired for their bright colors. Paired during the holiday season with a large splint basket full of balsam boughs, the arrangement will remain long after the holidays are over. Refreshing the greens as needed allows us to enjoy their fragrance throughout the winter months.

◀ The white-on-white farmhouse living room doesn't need the traditional red to express holiday cheer. A grouping of white poinsettias planted in old ironstone water pitchers is as festive as can be.

▲ An old hired-man's mirror that has lost much of its silvering rests on a stack of worn and discolored platters. The faded glass ornaments keep the mirror company with their similar patinas. A small boxwood wreath hanging over the mirror adds the finishing touch for this unconventional yet cheering holiday display.

A pair of cotton Christmas stockings hangs on a distressed blue and yellow painted door. The stockings are made from stretchy jersey cloth, antiqued in a tea bath, and filled with tissue paper to hold their form. They are a welcoming display on the front door or can be hung on the fireplace mantel in anticipation of Christmas morning.

▲ Tiny butter pats hold small colorful ornaments perfectly suited to them in size and scale. These holiday companions will be centered on each place setting at the casual holiday dinner table.

▲ Old blue canning jars hold mercury glass baubles. Arranged in a line on the kitchen shelf, these color-filled containers bubble with holiday cheer. A single white plate draws attention and creates a backdrop for the holiday grouping.

A hand-sculpted Santa, wearing a coat made from an old packing blanket with its stuffing exposed, welcomes a gentle hug from a mohair panda teddy bear. The unlikely duo embody the holiday spirit as they sit on the counter in the pantry.

Early mercury glass ornaments, gently placed in a bird's nest on the Christmas tree, celebrate nature as well as the holidays.

Spacious rooms allow for larger folk art displays during the holiday season. The blue-coated Santa hangs on the jelly cupboard in the corner of the carriage house great room, while an old wagon holds a newly made doll, teddy bear, and dollhouse. The tall Christmas tree hovers over all in the center of the fourteen-foot-high room.

A small Christmas tree in the carriage house kitchen is decorated with small antique medicine bottles. A tree light light placed in each bottle makes it glow like rich stained glass. The folk art angel hanging on the rustic board and batten door is made from antique quilt pieces and has blue and white coverlet wings.

◄I love the ocean, so seashells are never far from where I am. Here, a bowl full of surf-worn shells, collected over time, is decorated with a silver garland to celebrate the season while creating a shorelike feel in the Vermont farmhouse. Even though the beach is many hours away, the ocean is always close by in memory and spirit.

▲An ironstone milk pan, used long ago to separate cream from milk, now holds a grouping of freshly painted pinecones, presenting a pleasing contrast of glossy and barbed surfaces.

▲I always try to use fresh greens and real trees during the holidays for their scents and naturally organic appearance. But once in a while, I find something with such appeal I decorate with it as well. This artificial tree is a prime example. Casually planted in a common terra-cotta pot and placed at the window, it can be appreciated for its simple beauty in the room or from the outside looking in.

With a little bit of creativity, mundane items can become works of art. These ironstone plates seem to sway back and forth as they are cradled in my father's chicken feeder, salvaged from the barn. Plain glass ornaments roll into place in the foreground, adding some holiday flair.

▲ A dark green garden urn filled with seashells also holds sprigs of holly from the winter garden. The bright red berries add a pop of color to the holiday arrangement.

▶ A single red antique child's shoe glows on the balsam Christmas tree. The shoe, very unusual in color, was given to me by an old friend. Now prized as a special holiday decoration, it is packed away carefully each year only to be rediscovered and appreciated for its rarity and the generosity of the gift.

Bringing the outside in during the holidays is a refreshing and inexpensive way to decorate. Here, an old electric chrome teapot takes center stage as a quirky vase holding winterberries.

A small, weathered wicker basket hangs on a distressed pie cupboard. The bright red berries harmonize with the woody tones of the basket and cupboard while bringing holiday cheer to the room.

White ironstone pitchers, lined up in a row, display crimson winterberries. The ornamental twigs will last long after the holiday season. When they do fade, you can coat them with a harmonizing color of spray paint, giving them a contemporary look.

▶Fresh green wreaths usually hang on the front door during the holidays, but this one has moved inside. This densely made ring of mixed greens hangs on the jelly cupboard in the den and says, "Merry Christmas!" to all who enter the room.

◀A reproduction iron urn filled with balsam, white pine, and a few added twigs sits between the two vessel sinks in the upstairs bath. The fresh scents and bright green colors add Christmas cheer to this often overlooked room.

▼For a scent other than evergreens during the holidays, try fresh herbs. Rosemary sprigs from the local supermarket are tied in tiny bunches and hung along the mantel. A quick rub is all that is needed to release their fresh, pungent scent to mingle with the other holiday fragrances.

◀ Evergreens and forced bulbs add splashes of color to the kitchen and dining room. The juniper topiaries in the foreground, potted in clay pots and adorned with mica star ornaments, surround an antique finial from a mansion in Maine.

▲ An old European flowerpot carrier holds four festive juniper topiaries and pots overflowing with silver ornaments. This portable vignette is perfect as a tabletop display inside or out on the porch.

◄ Decorate wherever inspiration strikes. The everyday array of ironstone bowls stashed in this corner cupboard is adorned for the holidays with ornamental cedar boughs and colorful glass ornaments.

▲ A white corner cupboard in the dining room is dressed for the holidays. A small boxwood wreath placed on its door and a collection of seashells resting in a bed of greens are low-key but effective seasonal touches.